BLOOMS OF OLEANDER

BLOOMS OF
Oleander

By Steve Robertson

LIBERTY HILL PRESS

Liberty Hill Press
2301 Lucien Way #415
Maitland, FL 32751
407.339.4217
www.libertyhillpublishing.com

Printed in the United States of America.

Paperback ISBN-13: 978-1-6628-1698-7
Dust Jacket ISBN-13: 978-1-6628-1699-4
eBook ISBN-13: 978-1-6628-1700-7

PREFACE

O leander is pronounced ow-lee-an-dr. For those who are unfamiliar with oleander, please let me provide you with some background.

It grows as a small shrub, but it is far different than your average landscaping staple. Oleander has its own genus (Nerium). No one can say for sure what its land of origin is. It blooms year-round and is exceedingly difficult to eradicate. It is mysterious.

The oleander bloom also serves as an interesting metaphor for love. Its five-petaled flowers are quite beautiful and come in a variety of colors. They're also poisonous. If not handled properly, they can even kill those who touch or ingest them.

The femme fatale of the flower world, oleander provides a stark reminder that what's attractive to the eye might not be good for the soul. Simply put, the things you find irresistible could prove to be harmful. In some cases, they may be fatal.

I've been attracted to many things over the years. Some brought seasons of joy, while others brought the throes of wither. I've endured unrequited love, wasted love, and true love. My heart has run the emotional gambit.

It has been written that the heart wants what the heart wants. The ruin of many a young man has been following that line of thought. I share in that experience.

With every romance, I've learned something about life, love, and myself. I've shared time with lovers that brought both pleasure and pain. All those experiences were educational, and some were enjoyable.

My heart has been poured into every relationship I've chosen to take up. Those with whom I've shared time gave me a piece of themselves that lingers. I, too, left some of myself with them. At times, I wish I had those pieces back.

Those who took my heart and left it in slivers had their reasons. They were cold. They were cruel. They were blooms of oleander.

INTRODUCTION

S o why is a sportswriter penning a book of poetry? That's an interesting question. I have written three sports books and thousands of articles about the world of sports. I have had a lot of fun and sold lots of books. So why do something different?

The short answer is I love poetry and the freedom it brings. Poetry's cathartic for me. There are few hard and fast rules in poetry. It brings me a lot of satisfaction to take what is on my heart and share it with others. There is something magical about sharing your heart and other people finding a sense of kinship in your words.

The long answer is that in my mind, I'm always writing poetry. I enjoy the challenge of rhyming patterns. Poetry's like crafting a riddle with your most personal feelings and pulling that same emotion out of the reader.

At times, it is a little like torture. When I travel, my mind is always busy trying to create a few lines that make sense to me. When I share them with others, sometimes they make sense to them, too.

Poetry was like a first love to me. I love music, and I love the place great songs take me. This may be a little complicated for some, but music opens creative windows for me.

Great poems, songs, and stories are all out there in the ethos, just waiting for us to capture and share with humanity. There is a bit of commonality in that pursuit of artistry. It brings a spirit of community. When I hear or read something of beauty, I think, *I have felt that before, too.*

In the pages that follow, you will read things that my mind and heart have pulled from the ethos. I can't always explain where they come from, but I know that they're out there. I feel blessed to have been able to grasp some of that from the spirit realm and bring it to these printed pages.

Some of these poems are deeply personal. Some of it is cryptic. Some may only have meaning to me. My sincere hope is that you read my words and find some sense of connection. I hope that you can read along and find out that you're not alone.

I've had times in my life when I felt like music was my only friend. Music helped me heal; it helped me think, and it helped me feel a little more normal.

Isolation yields a terrible frame of mind. When I've found myself in the pits of my despair, the gift of music has often provided me with the strength to pull it all back together again.

This book is quite the departure from the things I have put into print before. Poetry's more of who I am. These are my words, and they come from my heart. I hope you find some inspiration, some joy, and some comfort in knowing that we live a shared experience.

We have all loved and lost. We have all been rejected. We have all had moments in our life where we felt that we could not go on.

On the other side of the emotional spectrum, we have had days when love was all that truly mattered. Through the peaks and valleys of my life, I've come to one firm, uncompromising realization. Love conquers all.

TABLE OF CONTENTS

Poems

Randoms

The Cycle of a Son

POEMS

Seasons

I know your heart is troubled. I would lend you what's left of mine if I could.

I will curse those who have hurt you and held you in place if it will do any good.

May the things that grieve you float away with the dandelions on the brawn of the winds of Spring.

When the memories and songs of better times cross your mind, may you find a voice to sing.

The boys of Summer seem to bring a smile to your face. May you always find victory in the battle of us versus them.

As your toes find peace in the wet sand, I hope the ocean breeze provides you with the calm spirit of requiem.

The Autumn tapestry in its brilliance reminds us that all things good and bad must come and go.

Change is the one sure constant in life and that is just as certain as the chill that comes when the cold winds blow.

Before you build a fire to warm you and yours as you yield to the annual coming of Winter's call.

May you soon realize that the things that torture your soul are really no trouble at all.

An Earnest Prayer

When they come for me and I know that they will, please let me be brave in my own defense.

For I have earned my enemies through no fault of my own, no umbrage or offense.

Allow me to demonstrate grit, character, and courage in the face of my ultimate demise.

I know that in the heart of my adversaries that my passing will serve as some coveted prize.

Dear God, permit me to die with my boots on for I am certain they will come from air, land, and sea.

Please give me a fighting chance, so that I can take some of those cowards with me.

CORNELL

In the days of my demise and admissions of powerlessness, your voice pierced the depths of darkness.

A tantric tongue roaring from the heavens to break the silence and solitude of medicated isolation.

As I wallowed in guilt and grief, your message found me with a ring of familiarity and kinship pushing me toward the light.

Words of comfort, inspiration and power began to take root in my soul. In time, they crowded out the weeds of fear.

The haunting timbre of your soulful sounds brought peace, grace, and serenity to my troubled spirit.

During the seasons of healing, I discovered that we were similarly afflicted. Brothers in arms with a common enemy.

I wish I could have stood alongside you to give you strength when the demons came to take you away.

You left this existence for Olympus and a Stargazer reunion, but your words will live in my heart in this life and the next.

The world is a darker place without you in it. My heart has searched high and low, but I have discovered that no one sings like you anymore.

ALMOST THE QUEEN

The run-off for high school homecoming queen didn't go her way.

That unfortunate outcome stayed with her long beyond election day.

While she was always so much more beautiful than the rest,

the opinions of others always made her feel second best.

As a small-town girl, she believed she had so much to prove.

She got her belly button pierced. Mama and Daddy didn't approve.

Oh, they did the best they could, but a wild child she would be.

Try as they might, no one could tame her. She simply had to be free.

She wore beat up boots and danced to the sound of steel guitars.

Even dropped out of junior college to go chase the southern stars.

A boy in a pick-up made her smile and convinced her to say, "I do".

Her mama signed for her to marry, even threw a shower at the church too.

He talked the good talk and promised to always stand big and tall.

In the end, she found out her good ole boy wasn't so good after all.

Tears of regret they came in bunches like water rushing from a fount.

Makes you wonder what could have happened if she had demanded a recount.

SONGBIRD

She flew in like a songbird out of the dark.
Her tune was pleasant and her beauty pure.

A feather or two may have been out of place,
but she was perfect to these tired eyes.

Fluttering in from the wilderness of heartache,
She wasn't lost, but clearly off course.

Careful not to spook her, I inched closer.
She carefully retreated but stayed in view.

The dance continued until fear abated.
Soon she realized I meant her no harm.

Finally, free from the cage that held her.
She found a home on the perch of my heart.

THE BREAK IN THE BEND

It seems that most of us consider life in linear terms. As if there is a straight line between life and death.

That's not really the case though. We have our ups and downs and rights and left before we lay down and take that final breath.

There is magic in wondering what comes next. The better part of the journey is not knowing the final destination.

I've had my share of unplanned detours on life's path. Those are where the important lessons are learned in my estimation.

Some days I run to see what's up around the corner, but other days I take the time to walk and enjoy the strolls.

The older I get the less that pace matters as I chose to take in the scenery of the hills, the valleys, and the grassy knolls.

I am grateful for the strength built from treading over unsettled and loose terrain.

I've found tremendous value in both the warm sunshine and the cooling rain.

The greatest part of the trek is the people I meet along the path.

When and why, they show up is hard to figure, but it's magic and not math.

We have no way of knowing how much longer we must shoulder this Earthly load, but I'm grateful to have found you here in this bend in the road.

A Place to Fall

If I offered up my heart would it be something you cherished or simply be another thing you took for granted.

Could you find the strength and the courage to make a move or are you too invested in where your feet are planted?

It is sad to consider that you would be willing to settle for a safe and convenient place to fall.

Why dine on half measures and meager portions when you could have had it all?

Our path is filled with choices, regrets, consequences, and rewards for all our actions.

There is no greater tragedy in life than trading true happiness for an existence spent starving on the fractions.

THE ANSWER

When I look back at how it all went. I often wonder if the time has really been well spent.

I've given my absolute all, but it seems to get harder to keep getting up when I stumble, trip and fall.

My heart fell into the hands of people who turned out to be less than I thought they'd be. In the end, they may actually prove to be the death of me.

I'd consider a deal with the devil for a love with angel eyes. I've already been through hell. Maybe he can sympathize.

I feel alone a lot, probably more than most. My only loyal companions are the memories of my friends before they all went ghost.

As I travelled through the land of revenge, I passed on staking a claim.

In the houses of the Holy, those who take vengeance are always held to blame.

Someday, I hope to sing the songs of jubilee. I wait for that glorious invite.

But if you asked me to spend forever here with you. You know that I just might.

It all gets so confusing but this you already knew. There are other questions you have of me this I know is true.

In your heart, you hold the answer, and you need no further clue. For no matter what else is said or done; Yes, I absolutely do.

Light On

I knew it was over long before you shared those painful words.

It was beautiful while it lasted but ended sooner than I preferred.

My spirit is nearly broken and my mind a complete and utter mess.

All I am left with are these dreadful feelings of pain and loneliness.

It's not just the loss of the moment, but of a future unfulfilled.

When it comes to moving on at peace, I am woefully unskilled.

I need to get up, get out and find something more productive to do.

I'm just pacing the floor and staring at the ceiling. I hate missing you.

The nights feel like an eternity and the days feel so terribly cold.

It's tough to find comfort when all you have is a memory left to hold.

While your spirit is filled with indecision and feels the need to roam,

I'll leave a light on hoping to help your heart find its way back home.

Mississippi Hippie

She wore silver jewelry and fashioned herself as a bit of a hippie.

She claimed to be a citizen of the world, but she had never left Mississippi.

She had all the classic records, but she didn't know the words to any of the songs.

She declared all her rights and had fun pointing out all my wrongs.

She tended bar at night and then slept most of the day.

She didn't wear much make-up, but I am not sure it mattered anyway.

She never got her hair trimmed and wore faded Levi's to every single affair.

She had a closet full of them at least a dozen pair.

She cooked Raman noodles for dinner like they were going out of style.

She had a way of making all the mundane things in life seem worthwhile.

She liked to lay in the middle of the floor and listen to the record player.

She said she believed in God, but never once folded her hands in prayer.

She told me that she loved me, but those words never really came easy.

She had a problem being honest. Intimate feelings made her queasy.

She felt totally alone in the world even when we were together.

She wore a coat to warm her cold heart even in warmer weather.

She drove me to face my consequences on Valentine's Day Eve.

She cried as she hugged me and swore that she would never leave.

She promised to write long love letters, but never found the time. She broke my heart in silence with no reason or rhyme.

BATED BREATH

Somehow, I've found a way to enjoy my life in the in between.

You know those moments that happen before the next big thing.

The beauty and joy in the day to day. Yep, that's just my scene.

I've learned to share my heart in the words I write, the songs I sing.

There is greater value in the people I know rather than the things I own.

This isolation, distance and uncertainty makes a nightmare of being alone.

The next chance we get to share some time I'm sure I'll need a moment or two.

For in my heart, I know when I get to breath you in that I won't be able to take my eyes off you.

I Got a Lot

Gotta lot of distractions that get me off track.

Gotta lot of things that I can't take back.

Gotta lot of people waiting to see me fall.

Gotta lot of reasons to say to hell with them all.

Gotta lot of pain that I just can't shake.

Gotta lot of defects most people can't take.

Gotta lot of folks who hate to see my face.

Gotta lot of motivation to ask for grace.

Gotta lot of blessings to be grateful for.

Gotta lot of scars, but I can wear some more.

Gotta lot of love in my heart to share.

Gotta lot of backbone for the burdens I bear.

Gotta lot of praying to do before I hit the light.

Gotta lot of feelings that hit me just right.

Gotta lot of people who say they're my friends.

Gotta lot of others that need to make amends.

Gotta lot of lovers who wish they had me back.

Gotta lot of friends who give me I what I lack.

Gotta lot of critics who have so much to say.

Gotta lot of proof they don't matter anyway.

Gotta lot of nightmares that came true.

Gotta lot of excuses to be blue if I want to.

Gotta lot of nerve to say what needs to be said.

Gotta lot of living to do before I'm dead.

Gotta lot of hard mileage on these feet.

Gotta lot of hits to take before I admit defeat.

Sojourner

We look quite different, but we are, in fact, very much the
same.
I felt a sense of kinship in your spirit before I even knew
your name.

You've learned those with hearts of gold can't get real love
from plastic people.
Not beneath the Summer sun, a haunted moon or even
a church steeple.

As a girl who would be queen you took a court jester's ring
as a love token.
In time, the most solemn oaths of the self-centered were
irreparably broken.

The bitterness of betrayal sent you spiraling in search of
new direction.
Fresh feelings of an unexpected freedom brought more
fear than protection.

Though it feels like your life is over and your heart is filled
with dismay,
You will gain the strength to take steady steps and soon
regain your way.

I offer these pearls of wisdom for I have been in your shoes before.
The gift of knowledge and experience is a gift to all who darken my door.

The path ahead is uncertain, and it is no place for the timid or the meek.
I offer no guarantees if it is eternal happiness and security that you seek.

Your journey is far from over and at times you'll want to give up.
When your spirit is tired and weary, come back to me. I'll refill your cup.

LIKE SAND ON THE SHORE

So much to say that feels important to me. Words and thoughts inside that ache to be free.

What looks so clear to me appears to you blurry. The time it's taking you to clear your eyes remains the biggest worry.

The object of affection for many with the thirst of the sun. There is no shortage of those wanting to be the only one.

I won't be satisfied being kept at arm's length. I know, without a doubt, that I am a source of true strength.

When it comes to you, my intentions are pure, so don't treat me like a symptom of the sickness when I am in fact the cure.

I am not just another grain of sand on the shore. I am the sea, and we will be as little or as much as you let us be.

Incubus

The angel on my shoulder was no match for the entice-
ments from this devil's daughter. I was powerless to stop
no matter how hard I fought her.

With the heart of Jezebel, she would make me feel like I
was in Heaven just before she dragged me through the
pits of hell.

She would make those now and again social calls with the
spirits of libation in pursuit of that tried and true, wicked
sensation.

Dangerous, but worth the risk she scratched a primal itch.
She had the playful look of the girl next door, but the heart
of an evil witch.

In her hands, she held a love that simply would not be
true. At her best, a lover that was borrowed that always
left me feeling blue.

It was more lust than love. More fun than fright. In the
end, we were simply two wrongs just trying to make the
night right.

LITTLE DO THEY KNOW

She doesn't talk about the past because it makes her sad. Her cheery disposition is a thin veil for the scar on her heart.

The sleepless nights are the penance and the penalty for doing her part from the very start.

A prisoner of principle, she lies awake on a pillow stained with tears born from obligation.

The paved road to happiness lies behind the locked gate of miserable complication.

They wrote it all off as some phase or emotional episode, but little do they know the pain will never subside.

Lost behind the words she can't bring herself to speak is the place where their ideal and her reality collide.

Like a slave chained to a fairy tale that won't ever produce a happily ever after.

She makes the best of it hoping she can hide her brokenness with a sly smile and forced laughter.

A Dream of You

I had a dream that you told me that you loved me. You looked me in the eye and told me there was no one else above me.

Continuing my slumber, I was able to fight off the daybreak. I guess I should be grateful for that sleeping pill I decided to take.

As I drifted under the spell of the sandman once again, I was able to see your beautiful face and your sly, toothy grin.

That moment didn't last. It was time to brush the cobwebs away. I had to pull the covers back, get moving and face another day.

You think you've got me all figured out, but things aren't always what they seem. I would trade it all in just to stay in that dream.

For now, I can only wish upon a star nestled high in the midnight blue and hope that someday my dream of you comes true?

In the Next Life

I am not sure that I believe in reincarnation, but if it's true,

then I feel confident I have known you before in a life or two.

A true conversance or sacred bond, for some reason I can't seem to place it.

We have loved each other in days gone by, even if you aren't ready to face it.

On the long nights when you have had more to drink than to say,

It's all the little things you do that just seem to give you away.

I rest assured knowing I have held your heart at some point in our existence.

Moving forward with love and care, I remain undeterred in my persistence.

You withdraw and use words of stubborn reluctance, but they ring hollow.

For I am determined to find you and love you in all the lives that follow.

MISSING

Out of sight and out of mind will only work for a little while,

but go ahead and tell yourself whatever you need to in order to feel better.

Lie and call it all a phase or something you were going through,

even though it was what you were looking for right down to the letter.

Sell me short and pretend what we shared didn't really matter anyway.

Memories of me won't be easy to erase and that gives me cause to smile.

You'll pass that little Mexican place out on the highway and think of me.

I'll be on your mind as you drive home counting every single country mile.

An old song of remembrance will come on the radio. You'll wish I was right there,

and I hope you get a lump in your throat that makes it difficult to sing.

When your eyes become wet with tears, I hope your make-up runs.

He'll ask you what's wrong and you'll turn and say, "It's okay, it's nothing."

But you and I, we both know different. Forever didn't happen for us.

You made your choice, so I guess there is really nothing left to discuss.

You're in someone else's arms and that's something that burns deep in my chest.

Of course, he'll never hold you the way I did. It'll always be second best.

PROMISE

Some days, I wonder what you look like in the mornings when the sun creeps in and shines light across your face.

What is the first thing on your mind as the last bit of slumber retreats and a new day gives chase?

I pray that pain and worry are far from your mind as you begin again each and every day.

May you greet the new dawn with gratitude and gladness knowing that all your greatest fears will stay away.

At some point, I hope I cross your mind and it brings a hopeful and happy smile to your lips.

May the director of your life's great play give me some important lines in the final act no matter how many times the script flips.

I don't know what you want with the rest of your life, but I hope you're able to afford and achieve all those things.

I may not be the one to give you a new last name or a shiny diamond ring, but I'll take you so close to Heaven that you can hear the angels sing.

Senses

Thankfully, the good Lord has blessed me with good health and the full complement of my senses. I am blessed in many respects. I offer no vain pretenses.

That said, if I woke up tomorrow and I could longer see. I would hope my mental image of you would be that time on Main Street when you couldn't help but smile at me.

If I stirred in the morning unable to smell the glory of the day. I would want the fragrance of your hair to linger and in my mind always stay.

I can't imagine losing the ability hear the music of the world. If I did, then the only voice I care to remember is that of a beautiful bright-eyed girl.

If my hands lose the ability to grip, feel and touch, I hope my mind can recall the first time I held you. Losing that memory would simply be too much.

If the sun rises tomorrow without me and I am no longer here, I hope that God will allow me to leave a few things behind to help you, my dear.

May you use my strength to help you stay on your feet when the battle is raging. Hopefully, it helps you to raise your sword in victory rather than defeat.

Take my vision in place of your own so when you see your-self in the mirror as I see you, you'll realize that you are worthy of the throne.

Use what's left of my heart and may it help you stand big and tall, because at the end of time there is only one pro-found truth and that is that love conquers all.

TROPHIES

They told me I was nothing, so I showed them everything.

They believed that I was weak, so I showed them true strength.

They thought I was all alone, so I built an entire army.

They underestimated me, so I made believers of them all.

They thought and hoped I would quit, so I finished the race.

They chose to become my enemies, so I made them my trophies.

TWO DOLLAR BILL

On their anniversary she handed him a two-dollar bill and said keep this as a token of our love. It is rare and unique like the bond that we share.

The man smiled sweetly, folded the currency, and slipped it into his billfold. He promised never to spend it even if down to his last dime.

As time went on, money got tight, and bills were high. She went into his wallet as he slept and took back her romantic prize.

Soon the man discovered his rare bill was missing and asked his bride where it might be. She soon confessed that the cupboards were bear and she had to spend it at the grocery.

Her husband went back to the store and worked out an exchange. He would stock shelves one week to have his two-dollar bill returned to him.

Once the week was finished, the grocer pulled out the same bill and paid the main for his services. Back into his wallet it went.

Weeks later, the man thumbed through his billfold in search of the precious gift. Long hours at work had him feeling lonesome.

As he reached for his bill in a moment to reminisce about the love he had won, he soon discovered it was gone once again.

Just as before, his bride had taken the money to buy needful things. The children required school shoes and they simply could not afford them.

The father went to the shoe store and offered to shine shoes for a week if he could simply have the two-dollar bill back.

After some convincing, the cobbler reluctantly agreed to allow the man to work off the debt.

The two men parted after seven days and the well-traveled bill was back with its proper owner.

The husband began to keep a closer eye on his wallet to ensure that he kept his two-dollar bill safe and secure.

One Sunday after church, the man panicked thinking he had tossed his bill into the offering plate. As his anxiety began to rise, his wife shared that she had taken it once again.

As the relief of the moment passed, the husband asked his wife why she couldn't simply tell him before she took it.

After all, the bill was a gift of some significance to the man as they were of meager means.

She screamed at him in anger and called him a fool for working extra hours just to keep the money when they had more immediate needs.

He calmly replied, "You gave the gift to me. You took it back and gave it to other men. Until I decide to give it away, it will always be my two-dollar bill".

Mama's Clinic

Just so you know, you rarely cross my mind. Chances are, these will be my final words to you.

You took me places I had never been before and made me feel things that were all brand new.

I told myself that you might be the one, but little did I know there was no value in the time we shared.

Sleepless nights and broken promises led to the realization that deep down you never genuinely cared.

Broken when I found you, you infected me with your sickness laced with lust and affection.

You pushed me so far from where I needed to be that any step taken would have been in the right direction.

Knowing you would hurt me and take everything didn't help. I was powerless to resist.

You left me with nothing not even a broken shard of my shattered heart big enough to slit my own wrist.

The suffering lingered long after joyous memories of you faded. Drugs and drink did little to numb the pain.

All new lovers were kept at a distance. I was determined not to let anyone near me cause any stress or strain.

Friends and family warned me about you. They said you would bring me sorrow and I believe I got double.

You didn't escape out the other side unscathed. Your sister told me that you got a wire hanger for your trouble.

I live with a ragged scar on my soul but make no mistake about it I don't ever miss you.

Sometimes I run my finger across that love and war wound grateful that I was simply able to survive you.

Needful Things

It's not in clothes, cars or keeping up with the Joneses.

It's not in dinner and a movie or a dozen red roses.

It's not in compliments, cheesy lines, or fake civilities.

It's not in special skills, hidden talents, or abilities.

It's not in hard work, a big career, or a hefty paycheck.

It's not in the tough times or any of those days when life is a wreck.

It's in those authentic parts of who I am that I put away on the top shelf.

It's in all the ways that I remind you to fall back in love with yourself.

SOMEDAY

Someday you're going to meet somebody you like better than me.

You'll struggle for the words, but you'll find them and leave me feeling empty.

I'll be left to consider if there was something left unsaid, or some romantic gesture undone.

Meanwhile, you'll have someone new to drink coffee with and have all your fun.

You'll make big plans and take grand trips together. There will be new pics of new adventures.

Gone will be any evidence of us. The old memories will be picked clean by emotional vultures.

He'll get to do all of things with you I wish I could.

Someday he'll even sit down and write you a poem like this one. It just won't be as good.

Oh, at some point I'll move on, but a piece of my heart will always be bruised blue.

I'll lean in to kiss somebody new, but she just won't be you.

Before he comes along and sweeps you off your feet and makes you feel like the queen to the masses.

I'm going to do all I can to distract you, so maybe you won't see him when he passes.

Farewell

Do not offer me in death what you withheld from me in life.

Save your false platitudes and sorry for your loss cliches.

If I was your friend, then treat me as such. Protect my name. Save it from slander and strife.

If you chose to be my enemy, then wear that distinction with pride even in my final days.

For I shall die as I have lived and that is without apology or regret.

When I reach the end, I hope to hold the hands of those I love and reflect back with pride.

If you won't wish me well then, bereft of me now as if we had never met.

I shall leave a piece of myself in the hearts I hold dear so that they may find me on the other side.

RANDOMS

S ocial media is a huge part of our culture these days. There are a lot of positives and negatives with that form of communication. I try to use my social media platforms for good.

I don't believe in tearing people down or getting involved in internet slap fights. As an old timer once said, "You're never going to beat a skunk in a stink contest." With that bit of knowledge in mind, I try to avoid the pitfalls of adversarial personal interactions on electronic mediums as best I can.

Several years ago, I decided to post a collection of random thoughts about the process of recovery. I got clean and sober December 10th, 1991. In the near 30 years that have followed, I have learned a few profound truths in life.

The fact of the matter is that every family will be touched by addiction in some way. I have gathered some experience, strength, and hope along the way, so I do my best to share that with the world.

It will never be about me or anything that I have done. I have a heart for the still suffering addict and all who love them. Doing my best to provide some hope for the hopeless and some proof positive that people can and do recover, the Randoms have become a regular part of my Facebook identity.

Many close to me have suggested that I write a book of Randoms. I am not sure if that will ever happen, but I decided to dedicate a section of this book to those who enjoy those random recovery thoughts.

Some may not apply to you, but my hope is that you will find some benefit in the words that follow. So here are some of the most popular installments of The Randoms.

Randoms-29

December 10th, 1991 was my first day of sobriety. Today marks the 29-year anniversary of that day. Here are 29 things I have learned along the way.

1. You must do it for yourself. People come and go in your life. If you do it for them and they bail on you, chances are you'll get loaded again.

2. You must realize that you're good enough. You must learn that you deserve a better life.

3. You must be honest with yourself and to others, but most of all yourself. The biggest lies we tell are those we tell ourselves.

4. You must be willing to make changes. I would have moved to Alaska and took up with the Eskimos if that's what it took. I would have done anything to get better.

5. You must know in your heart that your problems aren't just rooted in drinking or using. You have other hang-ups to address.

6. You must be committed to doing the work. No one gets sober by accident. You may stop drinking and using by circumstance, but that is not real recovery.

7. You need other people. No one recovers alone. It helps to know that someone else has felt the same feelings and battled the same struggles.

8. You must work the steps. Don't try and build a better mousetrap. Follow the plan and the program. Millions of others have found a new life one step and one day at a time.

9. You must take down the walls. Keeping other people at arm's length makes it hard to hug you when you're hurting.

10. You must commit to meetings. They are a reminder that we are not suffering alone and that we have people who understand. They are willing to help.

11. When I first got clean and sober, I still had to go to jail to pay my debt to society. My problems didn't go away. I simply dealt with them.

12. When I got out of jail, I had to borrow money to buy clothes. Just about everything I owned was lost in the hurricane of self-destruction.

13. When I went back to work, I had a boss that hated me. I kept showing up anyway. I needed the money. I dealt with it. I didn't like it, but I did it.

14. When I went back to church, some shunned me. Some whispered to each other as they pointed in my direction. I kept going. I wasn't there for them. I was there for me.

15. When I tried to date again, most parents didn't want their daughters to go out with me. I started dating out of town. They had pretty girls there too.

16. When I moved to Hattiesburg, it all felt right in the world. No one knew anything about me other than what I decided to tell them.

17. When I was hungry and broke, I used coupons and lived on bacon sandwiches and sweet tea for days at a time. I got my coffee at AA meetings.

18. When I felt like life wasn't being fair to me, I would go to a meeting and hear someone else talk about real problems. I learned to be grateful for who I was and what I had.

19. When I got too caught up in my own misery, I was redirected towards service work. I learned that doing things for other people made me focus less on myself and my own mundane problems.

20. When I got too full of myself and started to take too much of the credit, God gave me more of the work.

21. There are thousands of excuses to go get loaded, but not a single good reason.

22. The worst things that happened to me in my life happened after I got sober. I didn't drink. I didn't get high. I worked my program. I grew up. I took responsibility. I worked on acceptance.

23. No one can get me drunk or high other than me. It's my choice. I learned a new way to live and it gave me the ability to do what is best for me.

24. People have hurt me. People have surprised me with grace. People have conspired against me. People have offered their hand when I have stumbled. I have seen the best and worst in people. They are human just like me.

25. I didn't get lucky. I have worked for every single day of this. Some days have been easier than others. Some days have been so hard I had to remind myself to breath. They all counted the same, 24 hours. The sun came up the next morning.

26. It's been far from perfect, but man it's been fun. It's been educational. It's been as hard as hell sometimes. I have learned to be grateful for the days in the valley because I know I am headed back up the mountain soon enough. I just have to keep those feet moving.

27. I have worked a lot of jobs. I have been a lot of different things to a lot of different people. Above all, I have been my true self. I have been authentic. I can't stand myself when I must fake it. I might hurt your feelings, but I am going to tell you the truth.

28. I share sometimes that this is the best version of me there has ever been. I have never been happier with being me. When I first got clean, I didn't think much of myself. In time, I learned to like myself and eventually love myself.

I won't ever go back to being the person I used to be. The old me is dead.

29. Just about everyone that I got clean and sober with is either dead or back out riding the wave of addiction. That used to bother me, but the path is the path. I am grateful that I keep choosing this one.

Above all things, I am grateful. I am playing with house money. If life were fair, I would be dead. There was a time when I thought that would have been the better option. It isn't. The promises of AA have come true in my life. Everything I am, have or hope to be, are all a result of sober living. Life is beautiful.

One of my favorite phrases is "I didn't come this far to come this far". I must finish the deal. There is so much that I want to do, see, and feel. I have so many goals and dreams. I don't know when the good Lord will make the call and end the journey. Until he does, I am going to live wide open.

To the still suffering addict, I love you. You are not alone no matter what you tell yourself. I know. I was once in your shoes. If you're willing to be honest with yourself and take certain steps, then you can be in mine.

Randoms–Down

1. As an "old timer", I get asked what's the secret to staying clean and sober. I always sort of grin at the question. There is no secret.

2. The 12 steps are a simple and grueling process that saved my life. The hard part for me was doing what they told me. I tried to outsmart the process. It didn't take root for me until I stopped trying to find the easier softer way. I had to do the work.

3. As I have shared before, the worst things that happened in my life took place after I got clean and sober.

4. In my earlier life, I would have used that bad fortune as an excuse for self-destructive behavior. I would tell myself I deserved a drink or a drug. It was all nonsense I told myself to excuse my behavior.

5. I struggled through two babies dying due to miscarriage. I didn't get loaded over it either.

6. I laid my hand on my dad's arm as he took his final breath. I stayed with him out of shock until they came to take him away. I didn't want him to be alone. I kissed him on the forehead with tears streaming down my face. I didn't get loaded over that either.

7. I saw a company I gave my all for go belly up to bank-ruptcy. I wondered where my next paycheck would come from. I wondered if I could do anything else. I wondered if anyone else would hire me with my criminal record. I didn't get loaded over that either.

8. I had a friend and former roommate murdered. The sheriff's department never found any suspects. I believe they wrote it off as simply another dead dope head. He deserved better. I didn't get loaded over that either.

9. I have had my heart broken more times than I can count. You never get numb to that. It's the worst feeling in the world, but I didn't get loaded over that either.

10. I don't write these things to you in an attempt to praise myself or ask for any sympathy. It's simply evidence that people can and do recover.

The Big Book promises us that we will intuitively know how to handle situations that used to baffle us. That's come true in my life.

Here is the stark reality of life. Other people I love are going to die. People I love are going to disappoint me. Jobs will come and go. There will be injustice in life. That's all part of the human condition.

What I've learned through nearly three decades of sober living is that it's up to me. Bad things are going to happen to me no matter how "good" I am, but I decide how I am going to respond. That's my decision.

I have a choice today. You do too. This app on my phone says I've been sober, for 10,570 days. That's a big number, but the most important one was day one. That's the day I decided I had enough. That's the day I chose a better life.

It's not complicated. It's not easy, but as God as my witness it is so incredibly worth it.

Probably the most important thing I will write today is that getting clean and sober doesn't grant us any immunity in life. Bad things still happen. I just don't get loaded over them anymore.

Randoms–Heavy is the Weight that I Hold

1. When I first got sober, they told me I had to live life on life's terms. It took me years to figure that out. Simply put, getting sober didn't make me immune to the problems in life. They still happen to me. I just don't amplify them by getting loaded anymore.

2. There have been so many bad things that have happened to me. The path is the path. The Big Book tells me that God won't let anything happen to me that I don't have the tools to overcome. I am living proof of that.

3. When the storms on the sea of life have come and tossed me overboard, I have always had the strength to swim to shore. I no longer fear drowning. I just keep kicking.

4. Long term sobriety has taught me that I can't make the whole world's problems my own. There is a big difference between we have a problem, and you have a problem. I have a life to live too.

5. I have bad days just like everybody else, but I have learned that they are temporary. I am committed to a better tomorrow. I do my best to leave yesterday's issues in yesterday. Today's challenges will be difficult enough without trying to hang on to the trash of yesterday.

6. I had someone ask me a while back if I ever think about drinking. They were surprised when I said yes. I get hurt, I get angry, and I get mistreated. For a moment, those old voices demand to be heard. I just don't let them have center stage.

7. Getting sober is easy. Staying sober takes work, real work. It requires a daily renewal of all the positive things I did the day before. There is no easier, softer way.

8. Some days happiness comes in small doses. It's a message from a loved one, a picture of my granddaughter or a great song. Other days, I can't stop smiling. All sunshine and no rain makes a desert.

9. It's easy to stay clean, sober, and positive when things are going my way, but what happens when the tide turns? That's when I must work my program and use my support system. It's easier to do that when you actually want to stay sober.

10. I have shared this before, but the worst things that happened to me in my life happened after I got sober. Yet, I am still sober. I didn't get lucky. I didn't have a fairy godmother. I did my work, and I did what the old timers told me to do. I didn't drink.

There were times in my life that I felt I wasn't good enough. I felt like the world was against me and that I didn't deserve to be happy. All of that was based on lies I told myself. I don't listen to that trash anymore.

I read today that you must watch people who have survived all odds. People who have been able to come through the fire when it seems like the whole world was against them will not quit. I am cut from that cloth. I will not quit. I will not fail. I will not hang my head in defeat. I will rally the troops and come back with fire in my eyes. I will finish the deal.

I was blessed to be born with some of that. I didn't know how strong I was until I had to decide if I wanted to live or die. Over time I developed more skills and soon learned that there was nothing left to fear.

You can have that same level of courage. You can have that same warrior soul. The nonsense in your life ends whenever you're ready. Take up your sword and fight.

RANDOMS–IN A DREAM

1. It takes a tremendous amount of courage to change a life. Sure, there are circumstances that force some process of evolution, but it is so much more than changing jobs and addresses.

2. Yes, those are part of life, but you can still be the same person no matter where you earn a check or lay your head. There is a risk/reward component to everything but trading our authentic selves for the status quo pays little true dividends.

3. I spent years trying to live a life pleasing to other people. I guess in many respects I discounted how much people really loved me. There was a part of me that wondered if I would lose their love and respect if I did what was best for me. I was wrong.

4. If I had conducted an opinion poll, I could assure you everyone in my life would have voted against dreads and tattoos. All of that is cosmetic, but it is representative of who I truly am.

5. I had to be me. I had to do what I wanted to do. I had to do what I thought was best for me. What's funny is that I didn't lose anyone who loved me. I believe that they all love me more today than they ever have.

6. While you all see the hair and ink, what you don't see are the changes I made in my heart and mind. I became a different person, a better person. I became someone that I could be proud of. I found a place to plant my back foot and start handing out haymakers.

7. I found out that I like me and in time I learned to love me. I learned that I was capable of such great things. I learned that no matter what happens or what goes on, I am going to be okay. I will find a way to survive and thrive. It's who I am. It is what I do.

8. Without the decision to pursue my true self, there would have been no books, no show, no greatness, no true success, no self-confidence. In fact, I probably wouldn't be sober anymore. I stopped being a scared person fearful of being judged. I became someone I was proud of.

9. Some of the greatest regrets of my life have been the compromises I made to make life easier for myself. I used to let myself off the hook. I never held myself up to the standards I hoped to achieve. Sure, I worked hard, and I did the "right" things, but I was always holding back.

10. I say all of that to say this. A life lived to please others is awfully lonely. What DO YOU WANT? Figure that out and go chase it with all you have.

I know it gets complicated, but the solutions to many of life's problems are simple. We cloud them with our own cloak of fear. We might hurt some one's feelings, inconvenience someone or disappoint them.

When those people are dead and gone, we'll all be left with the life we built through our own decisions. It would be a shame to have lived life based on the approval of others. What happens when that's gone?

Those who love me have genuinely loved me through addiction, jail, rehab, all my character defects, the hair, the ink, and all the rest.

I know that anyone who absolutely loves me would not want me to live one more day under circumstances that make me miserable. I know they will always have my back no matter what I do or say and what I look like. Their love for me is not based on the status quo. It is because they love me and want what is best for me.

Having that in mind, the greatest freedom I have ever known is based on the knowledge that there is nothing left to fear.

Randoms–Into Dust

1. In the end, we are left with the sum of our decisions both good and bad.

2. What if we decided to trade in an "I just can't do it" for an "I want to be truly happy"?

3. What if the things we are trying so desperately to hang onto could be replaced with something better?

4. What if the comments from those who choose to concern themselves could be replaced with the song in our hearts?

5. What if we finally realized that those who are trying to hold us in place are doing so, because it's best for them? But what's best for us?

6. What if we're selling ourselves short, because it's the easier softer way? What if we're passing on joy for the sake of convenience?

7. What if the people and things we value only see us as a temporary solution? What if we are caretakers of dying flowers? What if we are wasting our precious water supply on things that won't bloom?

8. What if we could change it all tomorrow? Would we have the courage to accept and speak the truth?

9. What if we are held prisoner by our own fear disguised as something else? What if we stay under this false assumption forever?

10. What if we bet on ourselves and an uncertain future? What if we found something we never held or had before? What if we found liberty, freedom, and the things we dream of? Would you be willing to pay the price? Would you choose the mundane misery because it's familiar or strive for the life you truly desire and deserve?

What if?

RANDOMS–LIMITS

1. It has been a little while since I sat down and penned some randoms. My heart is in an emotional place today. I have had some phone calls with some people who are desperately trying to save a family member from addiction.

2. I am going to be frank, and I am going to share some things that perhaps the people who love you simply don't have the words to say. Being family sometimes means overlooking honest issues to keep the peace. That can be deadly.

3. Stop enabling negative behavior. You know it's wrong, but you allow yourself to be taken hostage and you pay the ransom too. Stop financially supporting alcoholics and addicts. STOP doing it! Stop today. Don't set a date. Do it now. If people have no consequences for their actions, then they will never change.

4. It is impossible to save someone without fear. If they don't fear the loss of relationships, stability, finances etc., then what if anything will ever change? You are bank-rolling their addiction. You are part of the problem. You are not helping.

5. A love without limits does not mean a love without boundaries. Establishing boundaries is part of that loving relationship. My family loved me enough to let me go to

jail. They loved me enough to let me go to rehab. They loved me enough to let me face my own consequences. They loved me through it all, but they didn't keep bailing me out. That decision saved my life.

6. Most of these stories don't have a happy ending. It takes a toll on me more than I can express in words. Each week, I talk to strangers about their inner most pain. I am honored that they feel they can share it with me. I try to prepare them for the possibility that their loved one may not make it. The odds are against them.

7. One of the most profound truths of recovery is that it is not just the alcoholic or addict that needs help. The addict and all who love them need help. If that means Al-Anon, professional counseling or a moderated clearing of the air, then so be it. All hold a part in the problem and the solution. Own your part without conditions.

8. When I was in treatment, a counselor told me that they were working with my mama to help her prepare to mourn my loss. I don't remember much of what they told me that day, but I remember that. It got to me. I don't think I realized my situation was so dire until Robert P. told me that.

9. For every person who suffers from chemical dependency there is a crisis, real or imagined, that is unresolved. There is some pain that they have been incapable of processing. Until that is addressed, the chances of recovery are near zero. It's not as simple as getting them off drugs and alcohol. We must resolve the underlying issue.

10. I speak with people about relapse regularly. The names change, but the stories are all the same. There is never any variance. "A.A. didn't work for me." I then ask a series of questions. Did you get a sponsor? Did you go to meetings? Did you work the steps? The answer is always no. Always, absolutely always no. It's not that A.A. didn't work for them. They didn't work for them.

You can't stop drinking and using and then just go back to the same life you've always led. Those same triggers, issues and problems will still be there. If you don't change them, then you will relapse. There can be no real recovery without a commitment to change. You keep hanging out at the barber shop, sooner or later you get the haircut.

So, it boils down to this. Do you want to live or die? It is that simple. There is no in between. The Big Book tells us that "we are like men who have lost their legs. We never grow new ones." We can never go back to being able to drink like a "normal" person. Those days are behind us. There is a new "normal" for us.

I can't promise you anything, but I can share my own experiences. I can say unequivocally that the promises of A.A. have come true in my life. I don't need to read a book or watch a movie. I have lived it. I have seen it happen firsthand. I am not special. I am not especially skilled. I did the work. I didn't get lucky. I took my second chance and never looked back. May you do the same.

I love you and I love all who love you. I know because I have been there. I may not know your name, but I know your pain. I know your shame, your guilt, and your desperation. My earnest prayer tonight is that someday you will know the happiness, peace, and serenity that I know now. You can have it. The choice is yours.

RANDOMS–LOVE SONG

1. Love comes to us in many forms. Sometimes it's a passionate kiss and other times it's a held door, a warm meal, or an affectionate hand on your arm when you're simply happy to be together.

2. Sometimes it's knowing when to hold quiet. Other times it's knowing what to say and when to say it.

3. Sometimes it's simply being there in those moments when words fall short.

4. Love doesn't harm, hit, or hate.

5. Love doesn't leave, lash or lecture.

6. Love is always on time even if it seems to be running late.

7. At times, I have confused love for lust, infatuation or simply the avoidance of loneliness.

8. Love is never work, but we often complicate it with expectations rooted in selfishness.

9. Love is never conditional. Commitment may be. Devotion may be. Togetherness may be. Love is limitless.

10. Love is the greatest of all things and when you truly have it in word and deed, there is nothing better.

RANDOMS–STEPPING STONE

1. I do not do what I do not want to do.

2. I am my own. I choose my steps. I make my own decisions.

3. No one can talk me out of what is in my heart and what I know to be true.

4. I refuse to be held hostage by anyone or anything.

5. I have chosen not to close the door on the past, but my course is set for the future.

6. There is so much more to life than just "raising kids and paying bills".

7. At times, I have been the dance partner of misery. Sometimes I was a victim, other times a volunteer.

8. It will never be alright until you make it ALL right. If nothing changes, then nothing changes.

9. The search party has been disbanded, the fire put out and the dogs placed on the wagon. You'll have to walk yourself out of the wilderness.

10. At some point, you must commit to making wishes a reality. Someday never gets here. Today is all we have. Why not make today the day to change everything?

There will always be distractions, excuses and those who want to hold you in place. It's easy for them to do that when they don't have to live with the consequences.

Those teardrops on the pillow belong to you. We have one life to live. May we all take full ownership of the days we have left. To thine own self be true!

RANDOMS–VOODOO HIGHWAY

1. I have learned a few things along the way. Sometimes I use this space in hopes of sharing some wisdom, promoting discussion, and finding a sense of commonality.

2. As I shared on *I Am Steve R* on Sunday, we are not always products of our environment. We are the sum of the decisions we make and the energy we produce. If you are getting back negative energy, then chances are you're attracting it.

3. The Lone Ranger's best friend was a person of color. Together they always found a way to save the day. They were equal partners in the friendship.

4. No one has ever risen to the rank of General without first learning how to be a good solider. We must put the work in and earn our rank along the way.

5. The best gifts aren't the ones with the big price tag. I have learned that things that require some thought and are difficult to get bring the biggest smiles no matter what they cost.

6. I have learned to be at peace with who I am. I don't need to pretend to be something I am not. That wasn't always

the case. I am happy being Steve for better or worse. I know that I can make the best of even the worst situations.

7. I am grateful for my friends. I am glad they see some sense of value in being associated with me. The older I get, the more I appreciate those who are willing to share some time.

8. Speaking of age, I know that there is less time ahead of me than there is behind me. That's a sobering reality. I have a lot left to do, but I have accomplished a big one. I used to have this big fear that I would lay on my death bed having never written a book. Working on number four right now. I won't have that dying regret.

9. I really miss my Dad sometimes. I think about him every day. I often wonder how he would feel about all that I have done since he passed away. I also know that God makes no mistakes. The path is the path.

10. I am still learning to be okay with other people being wrong. I feel like I have made a lot of progress with that over the years, but I still must fight against being the constant corrector.

In this day of social media, we are overrun with opinions, some good, some bad. Many of them are not rooted in facts. They're based on the cult of personality or emotional elevation.

Maturity has taught me that it's completely okay letting someone else have the last word and live in their own ignorance. That doesn't cost me a dime.

RANDOMS–YOU MATTER TO ME

1. I had a call tonight with a dear friend who lost a dear friend to suicide today. With that in mind, let me share some truths about me.

2. If you feel you owe me any apologies, know now that I don't need them. Any confusion or distance between us is only on your side. I want you in my life.

3. If you feel you owe me any amends, know now that I am open and available. I'm more than willing to talk and work through whatever it is. I want you in my life.

4. If you have wronged me, know now that I forgive you. I am quite capable of putting things in the rearview mirror. I want you in my life.

5. If you are unsure about where you stand with me know now that I love you. I want you in my life.

6. If you feel that you owe me any explanations, know now that I am all ears. I am ready to put it completely behind us. I want you in my life.

7. If you feel that you just don't have the words to say what you need to, know now that your actions mean more to me anyway. I want you in my life.

8. If you feel that the distance between us is too much to overcome, know now that I will meet you more than halfway. I want you in my life.

9. If you feel that things can never be the same between us know now that I believe we can build from here and make them better than before. I want you in my life.

10. Life is too short, and death is too certain to live with grudges, resentments and things left unsaid.

While I am human and I hurt, I have learned that a forgiving and kind heart serves me well. I use it regularly.

There is nothing that you have done, said, or thought that we cannot move beyond.

As God as my witness, I would rather have you in my life with all your faults, blemishes, problems, character defects and all the things you don't like about yourself, than to go on without a positive relationship.

I love you and if I haven't made it clear by now, I want you in my life.

THE CYCLE OF A SON

My dad, Freddie Robertson, was married three times and fathered four children. I'm the second and youngest child of that first union of matrimony.

Growing up in a divorced family is all I knew. I was just over a year old when my parents split. There were child support payments, visitations, and eventually stepparents. There were also a lot of things that didn't make sense to a young child.

Two houses, two Christmases, and two lives were things I grew to know. No one can explain why your family is different when you're a product of a broken home. You tell your friends, "I can't come this weekend. I'm going to my dad's."

The very first baseball game I got to play in fell on the first weekend of the month. Those were reserved for those trips to see my dad. I let it be known that I wanted to play and wanted my dad to be there.

Saturday morning came. I put on that #12 First Federal jersey with pride and couldn't wait for my dad to see me decked out in that canary yellow shirt with ironed-on numerals.

At eight years of age, I didn't have a high baseball I.Q. As Coach Jimmy Smith went over the final instructions, I asked him, "Coach, do they call strikes across the plate?"

Of course, they did, so I needed to be sure I kept a good eye on the ball all the way to the plate. I wanted my dad to see me get a hit. I wanted to make him proud and for him to know I was a good player.

I finally got the chance to bat. I remember being in that on-deck circle and looking up into the stands to see my dad sitting there. There was a real feeling of cognitive dissonance. He looked out of place. I was used to seeing him at his home rather than at the Westerfield baseball park in Columbia, Mississippi.

I should have been studying the pitcher, but my eyes were fixed on my dad.

When my time came, I banged my bat against my cleats before I stepped into the batter's box. I had seen my hero, Reggie Jackson, do that countless times. I'm not sure why he did it, but I did it because he did.

The first pitch evoked a gruff "strike one" from the umpire. Maybe it was nerves or fear, but it seemed like the kid was throwing pretty hard. His second pitch went into the dirt. The third went over the catcher's head to the screen. The count moved to 2-1. The next pitch nearly hit me, and I backed out of the box.

I began to remember what baseball announcer Vin Scully said on TV, "A walk is as good as a hit." As I considered the possibility of a base on balls versus a hit in front of my dad, strike two was called.

With the count full, my nerves were shot. Could I count on the pitcher to give me something to hit? Knowing that my dad's chances of ever being in the stands again were slim, I made up my mind that was going to hit the next pitch.

As the pitcher gripped that dusty pearl and sent it homeward, I swung as hard as I could. The ball sailed high, and I missed it for the final strike. I had swung at ball four. We went on to lose 4-3 to Terry's Small Engines.

I was less worried about losing than looking inept in front of my daddy. As he met me outside the dugout, he asked, "What are you doing swinging at a ball over your head?" It was the last time my father ever saw me play in an organized sporting event.

More games, more swings, and even some hits came, but my dad never saw them. He had to hear about them in stories I would tell on our visits.

In my final year of middle school ball, my team won the city championship. I wasn't there to be a part of it, though. It was my weekend with my dad. They won without me. I got to hear the play-by-play from my teammates at the end of the year swimming party. I still have that trophy they gave me around here somewhere.

I played football, but I was too small to be a real contributor. I found a home on the high school soccer pitch as a tenth grader. I was a starter as a junior and the team captain as a senior. We weren't particularly good, but we had a blast.

I even played some games close to my dad's home in Canton, but he never seemed to be able to make it. It hurt a little, but I had grown used to it. I played for the love of the game and my teammates. I told myself it didn't matter if I had no one to cheer me on.

On the junior college level, it all ended for me. I had been recruited by a few schools and had even picked up some partial scholarship offers. My high school coach told me that the folks at Jones County Junior College (JCJC) wanted me. My dad had gone there, so I went.

There were just two junior college programs in Mississippi at the time, that fielded a soccer team—JCJC and Hinds CC. Like most start-ups, things stopped for a while. The JCJC Bobcat soccer program officially disbanded not long after I arrived in Ellisville. I never played in another game where they printed the score in the newspaper. It's difficult to realize it when it happens to you until you're old enough to learn that chapter is over.

Years later, I married, became a father, and bought a house. I believe as you enter adulthood, you begin to see your parents as more of a resource. I never depended on my father financially once I was married. I guess I'm old-fashioned in that regard. If I had grown enough to make adult decisions, I needed to be man enough to pay for them.

Shortly after my first son, Oni was born, Daddy and I joked about us taking matters into our hands and that maybe Oni could lead our beloved Mississippi State Bulldogs to a Sugar Bowl. Then perhaps we could see State play in one during our lifetimes.

Like most young, first-time fathers, I was ready for my son to start walking, talking, running, and playing ball. As soon as he was old enough, we had him signed up for T-ball. I called Daddy and filled him in on the details, practice schedule, and a scouting report based on my observations of Oni during our front yard sessions. It was serious business.

The first day of team practice rolled around, and I think we were there an hour early. We had to stretch and get acclimated. All Oni wanted was a drink and a nice seat in the shade.

Practice finally got underway, and we were informed that we were the Indians. Oni was in a group of youngsters learning how to catch a thrown ball. It took him a couple of tries, but he got it down. A little later, he got to hit and run the bases.

Sometime during fielding practice, I felt a couple of tears hit my cheek. I said to my wife, "Just look at what all he missed." I didn't have to explain. She knew I was talking about Daddy. At that moment, I began to feel sorry for my dad and all the memories he didn't get to make with his boys.

It was a big step for me, and I think the first step towards healing an old wound. We got home from practice, and the phone was ringing. It was Daddy calling to hear how his grandson did in his first practice. It all seemed perfect.

The years went on, and Oni excelled in all sports. He was becoming an all-around athlete, and he had even taken up Tae Kwon Do. When Oni won the state championship for the first time, the first phone call I made was to my dad. I was anxious to share it with him. He couldn't tell you the first thing about the sport, but he knew his grandson was rather good at it.

In 2004, our family was in attendance as our fighter was competing in the Ft. Worth International TKD Tournament. It just so happened that the tourney fell on the same day as the Florida game against Mississippi State.

Daddy had become ill earlier that year, and by the time the Gators came to town, he wasn't attending ball games anymore. I called him every chance I got to get an update. We listened to the final minute with me standing outside in the only place I could get a signal. That day we didn't talk about doctors, tests, or treatments. The Bulldogs were playing and had won one for the ages.

Over the next few months, Daddy seemed to be doing better. When you have a loved one fighting a severe illness, your concept of time changes; you learn to take things one moment at a time. Each time we had something to feel better about, we made the most of it. Things were up and down for a while, and we just didn't know what was coming next. Life refused to stand still for us, so we did the best we could.

That following spring Oni won the AAU Tae Kwon Do Regional Championship for the third consecutive time. The Junior Olympics were held in New Orleans, so not having to travel far from our home in Baton Rouge and sleep in hotels we felt was a huge advantage.

The week of Junior Olympics, Daddy had to go back for some tests, but I did my best to focus on the road Oni had in front of him. Any worrying I did about Daddy's situation would benefit no one.

Junior Olympics brings together the best athletes in the country who could qualify as a regional qualifier. Being the regional champ again for Arkansas, Louisiana, and Mississippi, Oni was an automatic qualifier.

Tae Kwon Do Tournaments are usually comprised of two events—forms and sparring. Oni participated in Olympic style sparring his entire competitive career. During these Junior Olympic Games, Oni finished second in forms and third in sparring, which was good enough to find a place on the medal stand in both events.

After five years of coming home from Juniors empty-handed, our little guy won two shiny medals. Naturally, my first call was to my dad. Soon after I recounted every moment blow by blow, the line fell silent.

An awkward moment or two passed, and then Daddy informed me that he got the worst possible news from his test results. I'd like to say I handled it well and that I was faithful and true in my belief that all things work for good. If I did, it would be a lie.

I walked around my office angry. Our day had gone from the greatest ever to the worst possible.

I began to think about my son and his shining moment. How could I tell Oni today? What do you do when you don't know what to do? I did nothing.

I knew how horrible I felt and how unfair it all seemed. I wasn't going to pass that feeling along, so I kept the news to myself for a day or two until I could fully digest it.

Why my dad? Why now? He had just retired, and he had so many plans. He had so much left to do and several grandkids who needed spoiling in a way that only a grandfather could. I prepared then for the fight. Daddy wouldn't face this alone. We were all going to fight and pray right alongside him. We 'weren't going to just sit around feeling sorry for ourselves. Daddy would never approve of such.

There was not a lot of encouraging news the rest of the way. As things began to wind down, I began to ask myself specific questions. What could I do? Did I owe Daddy any amends or any apologies? Had I told him I loved him enough over the years?

I think it hit me somewhere around the Lexington, Mississippi exit as I headed down I-55 south. I knew what I had to do. I knew what I owed him, and I knew I had to speak with him. I made plans to stop by the hospital on my way home, but when I got there, I chickened out. I chickened out three more times before I finally said it.

Once Daddy was in his final days, and I had come to be by his side for the duration, I finally got the courage up to tell him what I needed to say. We were all standing around his bed telling funny Daddy stories, and I just grabbed his hand and let it go.

"Daddy, I don't want you to ever think that I got the short end of the stick. I don't want you to ever think that I never knew how much you loved me. I know we both made some mistakes along the way, and I think we made up for them as we got older. I know you did the best you could, and I love you for it. I know you wanted to come to see me play ball all those years. I know you wish you could have, but I want you to know I got over it a long time ago. When I became a man with a wife and family of my own, you became my best friend."

I get misty-eyed just typing the words again. He couldn't talk anymore, so he couldn't respond. He didn't have to. I could tell by the look in his eyes that I had unburdened him. I had freed us both. It was something we never talked about, but it was something that ate away at both of us.

Now, it was behind us. As I scanned the room, there wasn't a dry eye in the place. I slept that night like I never had before. I was exhausted. The emotion of it all weighed on me more than I ever realized. I knew then I could let him go with no regrets.

The final words my Daddy said is something I will never forget. With his wife and their children all around his bedside, he cleared his throat and said, "I love all of y'all." Again, my eyes are watering as I type.

I've thought more times than I can remember that there could never have been a better final statement from him or anyone else for that matter.

In the end, love for each other is all we have, and we realize it's all we ever really had in the first place. When my daddy left this world, I was there with him holding his hand. I count that as one of God's greatest gifts to me.

There were times after that I'd say out loud, "I can't do this. Going on without him is too hard." As soon as I'd get those words out, I could hear him say, "You don't have a choice. You have to."

The fall of my daddy's passing, I played soccer for a men's team for the first time in over a decade. I wasn't in excellent shape, and I had lost a step or two, but the competitive juices still flowed. My dad died just before our first game.

After he was gone, I felt like he was always with me and always watching me. So, I became cautious about my behavior. I didn't want him to see me doing anything that wouldn't make him proud.

The night of our first game, my wife came to the game and brought all four of our kids, so they could see their daddy play. I was hoping to avoid embarrassing myself.

The first half was rough, and I felt older than ever. I was nowhere near the player I used to be, and I was hard on myself about it. I looked around, and those other guys seemed to be a step ahead of me every time. I was tentative.

At halftime, I had a little pep talk with myself, and I asked to go back in. I ended up playing left wing. It wasn't my spot, but I was glad to be out there.

About three minutes in, a crossing pass came from the right-wing, and I timed it exactly right. BANG! BANG! It was in the back of the net. As soon as the ball hit the nylon, I was overcome with emotion. I turned and pumped my fist and pointed to the heavens.

I said, "Daddy that was for you. I'm glad you finally got to see me play." I didn't score another goal the rest of the year, but of all the ones I did in my life that one means the most. My kids thought I was the man, and I got to fill a need within myself. It was a great moment.

If State was playing, I knew Daddy was watching or listening to the ball games. I smile to myself sometimes when I think that Daddy doesn't have to listen to the broadcast anymore, and he doesn't have to worry about what's happening when the commercial breaks run long. He gets to see every game live without commercial interruption, including the ones his grandkids play in. There are so many things I wish I could talk to him about if I had the chance.

If we talked about things in life that sometimes seemed unfair to me, he would tell me in his Jones County raised voice that everything would be alright one way or another and that the rain falls on the heads of the just and the unjust alike.

He would find some way to poke fun at me for being able to wear his suit after being such a bean pole most of my life. I'd tell him that I may be able to fill his suit, but never his shoes.

I'd tell him that his grandsons are all playing ball, those who are old enough. We're still working on that Sugar Bowl, and since he's in closer contact with the folks who affect such decisions, please put in a good word on our behalf.

The main thing I'd want to tell him just one more time is that I loved him, and everything I am or ever hope to be in this world is because of him.

Freddie Robertson is the greatest man I have ever known, and every person he knew was a better person because of him.

Mississippi State sports brought daddy and me closer together. We became best friends again because of the Bulldogs.

Some of my most incredible memories are going to games with him. If we were apart from each other, I'd always call him before, during, and after games. It gave us a closer bond.

If you can make that call to your father, go, and make it now. One day that option will no longer be available to you. If there are any unresolved issues, then get them resolved now. Life is too short, and death is too sure to live with that. At least that's what my daddy told me.

ACKNOWLEDGEMENTS

Thanks to: Dana, Oni, Betsy, Vivi, Audrey, Mia and Ian for putting up with me. I am not sure many people know how many hours they spend away from me. I am either covering a ball game, on the road signing books or up in my office pecking away at this keyboard.

Special thanks: Paul Brown & Suezette Hankins. They both do an awful lot to make me look good. Neither of them, ask for any credit.

Much love to: Pat & Stephanie Robertson, David & Kim Kennedy, Mark & Nikki Smith, Gordon & Tara Foil and William & Regan Lunceford. Chad & Sandy Palma and Eric & Mandy Wilshusen. They are my siblings and I love them all. Their kids and grandkids are all special to me.

Deepest appreciation: Brandon Sullivan, Jade Gaskin, Sam Denton, Carolyn Abadie, John Evans, Jay Yates, Stan Raye and John Hendricks.

God bless the family of Chris Cornell.

Finally, thanks to all who believe in me and to all of those who don't. You have both motivated me to be the best that I can be.

CPSIA information can be obtained
at www.ICGtesting.com
Printed in the USA
LVHW082131280521
688849LV00017B/659/J